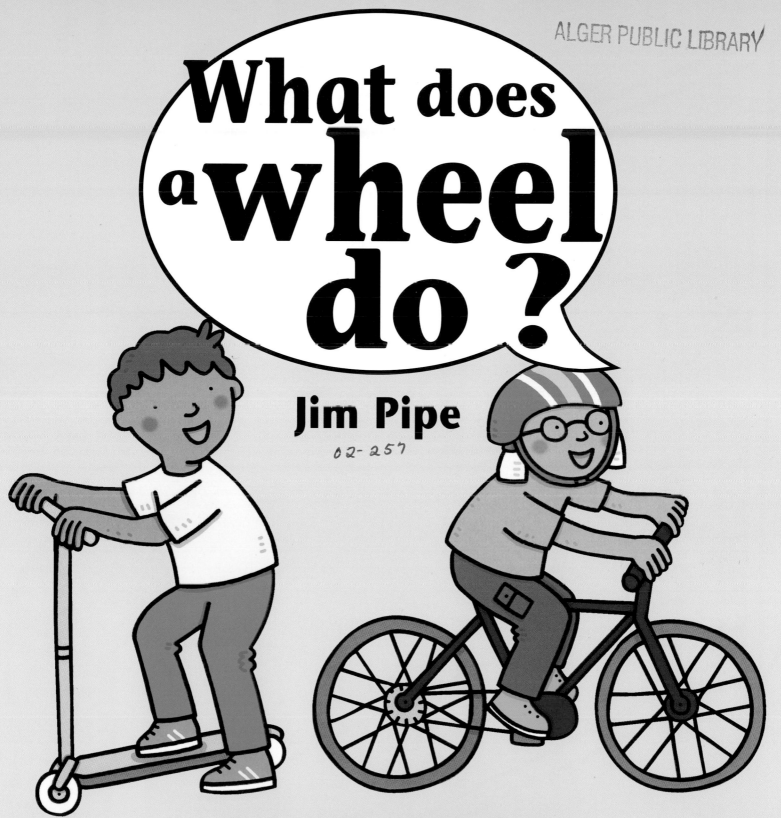

What does a wheel do?

Jim Pipe

Copper Beech Books
Brookfield, Connecticut

Does it roll or slide?

Zack's dad is driving Zack, Jo, and Amy to Steve's house. On the way, they stop at a gas station. Out of the window, the children can see a woman moving a barrel.

2

3

Let's see how the children find out.

Why it works

Shapes with a flat surface slide. Shapes that roll have a round surface touching the ground. But a barrel or a can has a flat side and a round side, so it rolls or slides.

Solve the puzzle!

Can you tell what rolls and what slides? Make a slope using books and a wooden board. Then find a marble, a book, and a pencil. Put them on the slope and write down whether they roll or slide. Check your answers on page 22.

Why is a wheel round?

At Steve's house the children go into the yard to play. Steve whizzes around the yard on his scooter. Amy takes a ride on Steve's bicycle.

It's easy to whiz around on wheels!

7

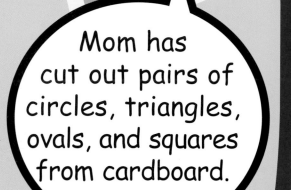

1

Let's see how the children find out.

2

Mom has cut out pairs of circles, triangles, ovals, and squares from cardboard.

The triangles and squares keep getting stuck!

Let's tape each pair to the ends of a straw.

3

8

Why it works

If a shape has corners, like a triangle or a square, you must lift it to roll it over. Round shapes don't have corners, so they roll smoothly. A circle rolls the best because its shape is the same all the way around. But an oval is flatter in some places than others, so you also need to lift it up and over to make it roll.

Solve the puzzle

Does a ball roll like a wheel? Think about the different shapes of balls and wheels.

9

Why do you whiz down a slide?

Steve has a great slide in his backyard. Jo goes whizzing down. But when Zack tries to slide down the grass hill, he slides very slowly.

11

Let's see how the children find out.

3

Let's try it on this mat. It is rough like grass.

Now it needs more marbles to make it slide. Things must slide more easily on a smooth surface.

Why it works

When one object slides on another, bumps on their surfaces rub against each other. This keeps them from sliding so easily. Even a very smooth surface is covered in tiny bumps. But a rough surface like the mat or grass has bigger bumps than a smooth surface, so it is harder to slide on.

Solve the puzzle

Do things slide more easily if they get heavier? See how many marbles it takes to make an empty box slide. Do you need more or fewer marbles if you put in a heavy book?

13

What does a wheel do?

The children play in Steve's wagon. They take turns pulling each other around the yard. Steve can pull the wagon even when both Amy and Jo are sitting in it.

I can pull both of you in my wagon!

15

Let's see how the children find out.

16

> The pencils lift the book off the table. Only a small part of each pencil touches the table, so the surfaces must only rub a little.

Why it works

Wheels and round pencils make it easier to move things because rolling is easier than sliding over bumps. Look closely at a wheel and you will see that only a small part of it touches the ground, so there is a lot less surface for the ground to rub against.

02-25 7

Solve the puzzle

Do wheels always roll? Think about what happens when a bicycle or car stops very quickly.

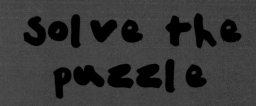

3

What makes us slip and slide?

The children are taking turns being "it," and chasing each other around the yard. But when Jo runs onto a wet patch of grass, she slips.

Are you OK?

I'm fine. I think I was going too fast.

You weren't going that fast. Are your shoes smooth on the bottom?
Jo was fine on the path. I think she slipped where the grass is wet.
What do you think?

Let's see how the children find out.

Look, it takes fewer marbles to make the box move, and it just keeps sliding!

Why it works

Water between two surfaces stops them from rubbing against each other. That's why water can make things slippery. Oil works in the same way. Oil is put in car engines to stop the parts from rubbing against each other.

Solve the puzzle

What stops you from slipping when the ground is wet? Think about the bumps and grooves on the bottom of your sneakers.

Did you solve the puzzles?

Can you tell what rolls and what slides?

Look at this chart and check your answers:

Rolls	Slides
Marble	Book
Pencil	Pencil

A pencil rolls or slides, like the can on page 5. It rolls on its side, but slides if you point it down the slope.

Does a ball roll like a wheel?

Most balls are circle-shaped all over, so they can roll in any direction. Footballs have an oval shape, so they don't roll well end over end. A wheel is round on just one side, so it can only roll forward and backward.

Do things slide more easily if they get heavier?

No, the heavier something gets, the harder it is to make it slide. So if you put a heavy book inside the box, you will need more marbles to make the box move (below).

Do wheels always roll?

Wheels are round, but they do not always roll. If a bicycle or a car stops very quickly it can slide. When this happens, it skids. Fast cars often have wide wheels to stop them from sliding so easily.

What stops you from slipping when the ground is wet?

The bottom of most sneakers is covered with bumps and grooves. These stop the shoes from sliding easily, even when it is wet. Cars and bicycles have grooves on their tires for the same reason.

23

Index

© Aladdin Books Ltd 2002

Designed and produced by
Aladdin Books Ltd
28 Percy Street
London W1T 2BZ

First published in
the United States in 2002 by
Copper Beech Books,
an imprint of
The Millbrook Press
2 Old New Milford Road
Brookfield, Connecticut 06804

ISBN 0-7613-2722-3

Cataloging-in-Publication data is
is on file at the Library of Congress.

Printed in U.A.E.
All rights reserved

Literacy Consultant
Jackie Holderness
Westminster Institute of Education,
Oxford Brookes University, England

Science Consultant
Michael Brown

Science Testers
Ben, Toby, and Elliott Fussell

Design
Flick, Book Design and Graphics

Illustration
Jo Moore